MW00883438

IS BORIS

Life of Boris Cookbook
© Life of Boris
© Double Decaf
Text: Boris B. Blinkov
Illustrations: Double Decaf

2024

Boris B. Blinkov

LIFE OF BORIS
COOKBOOK

Illustrations DoubleDecaf

Salty

Sweet

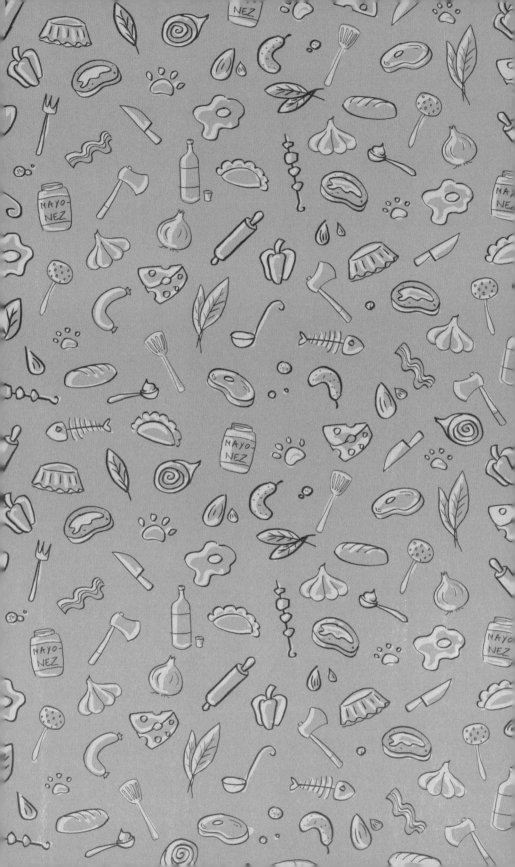

Salty

Goulash

just like mama makes it

🕐

prep:	20 min
cook:	2.5-3 h

ingredients:

- 1 kg / 2.2 lb good beef
- cooking oil
- 1 big onion
- 2 tbsp sugar
- 2 cloves garlic
- 2 tbsp paprika powder
- 1 tbsp tomato paste
- 1 tbsp garlic powder
- 2 tsp cumin seeds
- water
- salt
- black pepper
- 2 bouillon cubes
- bay leaf (or maybe two)
- half cup wheat flour
- 1 tbsp marjoram

USE A SEPARATE CUTTING BOARD FOR RAW MEAT!

also needed:

- cutting board & knife
- pan for frying
- large pot for cooking
- bread and butter for buterbrod

instructions:

1. cut beef into cubes. put some oil on pan and fry beef until slightly brown. put fried beef aside into pot.

2. slice onion and fry on pan until brown. lower the heat and add paprika powder, sugar, fresh garlic, cumin, garlic powder and tomato paste. fry on low until fragrant. add the mix into the pot with meat. add water on top until components covered. cook on medium heat for 30min **.

3. now add the bouillon cubes, salt and black pepper. cook on medium heat for 1h. take this time to make some buterbrod. after that add the bay leaf ... or maybe two!

4. dissolve flour with some cold water to make a slurry. pour it into the pot and mix well until sauce starts to thicken. add the marjoram. cook on low for another hour.

5. serve with diced raw onion on top and mayonez on the side! do not forget the buterbrod. enjoy!

watch the video

**remember to guard from neighbour Vadim

End of month ukha

big flavour for little money

difficulty: gopnik

🕐

prep: 20 min
cook: 30 min

ingredients:

- 2 L / 8.5 cups water (don't use river water)
- 1 medium sized freshwater fish
- 1 large potato or 2 small ones
- 1 onion
- 1 carrot
- green onion
- parsley
- dill
- bay leaf
- salt and pepper

also needed:

- big pot
- bayonet or good kitchen knife
- cutting board
- vodka and semechki
  to pass the time

For best result use freshwater fish

instructions:

watch the video

1. build a fireplace outside or use kitchen if being fancy.

2. catch fish.

3. gut fish but keep fish head for great flavour. use all parts of fish (except guts) for best taste. but you can take out bones if don't want toothpick soup.

4. cut vegetables into bite-sized chunks. precision cutting not necessary.

5. add water and all ingredients into a big pot. cook for 30 minutes until vegetables are soft.

6. enjoy with a side of bread or cheburek.

Milk soup

a hearty soup or a challenging drink

ingredients:

- 250 ml / 1 cup uncooked pasta
- 500 ml / 2 cups water
- 500 ml / 2 cups milk
- 1 tsp salt
- 2 tbsp butter
- 2 tbsp sugar

also needed:

- pot
- spoon

USE FULL FAT MILK FOR BEST RESULT

instructions:

1. set 500 ml / 2 cups of water to boil. add salt. when water is boiling, add pasta and boil until almost ready. don't pour out pasta water, it will make a heartier soup.

2. pour milk into the pasta pot. mix in sugar and butter. simmer on low heat for a few more minutes until pasta is cooked.

3. serve right away with a side of buterbrod. enjoy!

works with any pasta shape

watch the video

Chebureki

pretty much a big fried pelmen

ingredients:

dough:
- 1 egg
- 400 g / 3.5 cups flour
- 1 shot of vodka
- 1 tbsp sugar
- 1 tsp salt
- 200 ml / 1 cup water
- 2 tbsp sunflower seed oil

filling:
- 400 g / 14 oz minced beef or pork
- 2 small onions
- 1 clove garlic
- 1/2 tsp pepper
- 3 tsp salt
- green onion
- parsley
- dill

also needed:

- 2 bowls
- cutting board & knife
- rolling pin
- frying pan or deep fryer
- paper towels
- 1 L / 4 cups sunflower seed oil

16

watch the video

instructions:

1. mix the flour, egg, salt, sugar, water and oil in a bowl. add an optional shot of vodka. mix dough by hand for best effect.

2. put minced meat in the other bowl. chop onion and garlic into small pieces and add into the meat bowl. season with salt and pepper. chop up and add some parsley, green onion and dill. mix by hand!

 don't forget to wash hands after handling meat!

3. divide the dough into six equal parts. on floured surface roll out the dough into circles.

4. place a tablespoon of meat mix in the center of dough. fold dough over the meat and close with fork.

5. fill pan halfway with oil and heat up. deep-fry on each side for 2-3 minutes. leave to rest on a paper towel.

6. serve with mayonez.

7. enjoy!

17

Cabbage rolls

a Slav multitasking challenge

difficulty: babushka

prep: 1 h
cook: 2 h

ingredients:

- 1 whole cabbage
- 100 g / 0.5 cup uncooked rice
- 400 g / 14 oz minced meat
- 2 onions
- 4 carrots
- 4 cloves garlic
- salt and pepper
- tomato sauce
- water
- bay leaf
- dill
- sour cream
- mayonez

this recipe requires use of 6 hands and brain on caffeine rush. or if you are babushka, then you can do this as a side project while doing laundry by hand.

also needed:

- big pot for whole cabbage
- cutting board & knife
- medium pot for rice
- pan
- oven pot

instructions:

slice off thick spine on cabbage leaf for easier rolling

1. fill big pot half way with water. bring to boil. set another smaller pot to boil for rice.

2. prepare cabbage. take off top leaves and cut out the core. put whole cabbage in boiling water. boil 7-10 minutes under a lid. peel off cabbage leaves and let cool down. if inner leaves are too stiff, boil cabbage for another 5 minutes. at the same time keep eye on rice. don't overcook, it should be still hard inside. strain rice.

3. cut onions into small pieces and grate carrots. crush garlic. fry all on pan until light brown. put in a big bowl. add the boiled rice, raw minced meat, salt and pepper to same bowl. mix it good.

4. now start rolling. take some filling and put on cabbage leaf. fold the sides and roll. repeat.

5. put some oil in oven pot. place cabbage rolls in the pot seam side down. stack as many in the pot as needed. pour some leftover cabbage water in the bottom to not burn the rolls. cover with lid. cook cabbage rolls at 200°C / 400°F for 1.5 to 2 hours. in the mean time warm up tomato sauce on pan. don't forget the bay leaf.

6. serve cabbage rolls with tomato sauce, sour cream and of course mayonez. add fresh dill on top, congratulate yourself on passing the slav multitasking challenge and enjoy!

watch the video

Stroganoff

beef coctail
with onions and mushrooms

difficulty: Boris

🕐

| prep: | 15 min |
| cook: | 30 min |

ingredients:

- potatoes from babushka's field
- 400 g / 14 oz beef
- 2 onions
- 3 cloves of garlic
- some mushrooms
- butter (not margarine)
- salt and pepper
- 1 tbsp flour
- 500 g / 2 cups sour cream
- some mayonez to borisify
- bay leaf
- green onion

also needed:

- pot
- pan
- cutting board & knife
- shot of vodka

instructions:

guard from neighbour Vadim !

1. wash mud off potatoes. leave peel on for more rustic flavour. set potatoes to boil in pot.

2. cut beef into thin slices. chop onion and garlic into small pieces and mushrooms into bigger pieces.

3. heat up a big pan. throw in some butter and fry beef until brown on sides. don't crowd the pan unless want boiled meat. fry beef in batches if necessary. add salt and pepper. set fried beef aside in a bowl.

! don't wash the pan after frying meat you're wasting good flavour!

watch the video

4. on same pan fry mushrooms in butter. after the mushrooms have shrunk down to half their size add onions and garlic. fry until caramelized. mix in flour and fry a little more.

5. add the fried beef back to the pan. pour in a shot of vodka for strength. then pour one on the pan too. add sour cream and bay leaf. mix. cook for 10 more minutes.

6. stab potatoes. if knife goes through easily then is ready. otherwise give it a few more minutes. drain.

7. serve with pickles on the side and let green onions fall from heavens. enjoy taste experience of your life!

Shashlik

pork bits on a stick à la Boris

ingredients:

- 1 kg / 2.2 lb pork neck
- olive oil
- vinegar
- soy sauce
- spice mix (optional)
- salt and pepper
- lemon juice
- 2 onions
- 2 garlic cloves
- mayonez and ketchup

also needed:

- big bowl
- cutting board & knife
- shashlik swords

watch the video

instructions:

1. cut pork into fairly big square pieces.

2. in a big bowl mix olive oil, vinegar, soy sauce, spice mix, salt, pepper and lemon juice. the amounts depend on your preferences. taste it. there needs to be enough liquid to almost cover the meat.

3. cut 1 onion and the garlic cloves into pieces. no precision cutting needed. add them into the marinade.

4. add meat into the marinade and mix it through with your hands. cover the bowl with something and throw it in the fridge to marinate for 2-3 days.

5. take out shashlik from fridge. let come to room temperature while you make fire.

6. impale pork bits on skewers. for more flavour impale some onion quarters between meat bits.

7. throw full skewers on grill. coals should be glowing hot but not burning with flame. you are not trying to make more coal. grill for 10-15 minutes, depending on how hot the coals are.

8. enjoy with mayonez, ketchup or just as is!

Borsch

Slav up your life

prep: 30 min
cook: 40 min

ingredients:

- 1.5 L / 6 cups water
- 1 medium size beet
- 2 potatoes
- 1 carrot
- 2 small onions
- half a cabbage
- 2 garlic cloves
- shots of vodka (optional)
- 300 g / 10 oz meat with bone
- 1-2 bay leaves
- salt and pepper
- sour cream and dill for on top

also needed:

- pot
- pan
- cutting board & knife

instructions:

1. cut meat into big pieces. put in pot and cover with water. set to boil for 1.5 hours. skim off the scum that floats to the top. use water from meat as soup base. optionally use meat in the soup for best taste.

2. cut the boiled meat, raw beets and potatoes into bite size pieces. add them to soup base. add 1.5 L / 6 cups of water. set it to boil on low temperature. don't forget the bay leaf!

3. cut up carrots, onions and garlic. fry until golden brown for more flavour and add to the soup.

4. add salt to taste. add some pepper too.

5. cut up the cabbage and add to soup.

6. boil until all components are soft to eat.

7. serve with black bread, sour cream and dill on top.

watch the video

25

Languguette

in sour cream sauce

difficulty: Boris

prep: 30 min
cook: 1.5 h

ingredients:

- 400 g / 14 oz beef
- 200 g / 1 cup sour cream
- 2 tbsp mayonez (Boris edition only)
- 300 ml / 1.3 cup hot water
- 1 onion
- 2 bay leaves
- 2 tbsp pig fat
- 3 tbsp flour
- 2 tsp salt
- 0.5 tsp ground black pepper
- lemon juice

also needed:

- pot
- pan
- cutting board & knife

LANGUETTE...
LANGUETTE...
TONGUE???
WTF IS THIS RECIPE!?

watch the video

instructions:

1. cut meat into tongue shaped slices. beat the meat with a meat mallet or fist if frustrated. squeeze lemon juice on top and let marinate for 10-15 minutes.

2. cut onion in slices. add a generous amount of pig fat on pan and fry onions on medium heat until soft. set aside.

3. in a bowl or deep plate mix together flour, salt and pepper. dip meat into flour and cover both sides generously. fry on pan until golden brown. fry meat in batches. add more pig fat if pan is getting too dry. flour coating soaks up fat.

4. add all fried meat and onions back on pan and set to low heat. in a small pot boil water and carefully pour it into the pan. remember, hot oil + cold water = BOOM.

5. cover the pan with lid and simmer for 1-1.5 hours until meat is tender. if necessary add more boiling water during cooking. while meat is cooking, boil potatoes.

6. towards the end of cooking take meat slices out of the pan and set aside on plate. add sour cream, bay leaf and mayonez on pan. mix well. put meat slices back on pan and simmer for another 10 minutes.

7. serve with potatoes and cucumber slice.

8. bon appétit mes camarades!

Kotlet

just like babushka makes it

difficulty: Boris

prep: 20 min

cook: 10 min

ingredients:

- **400 g / 14 oz minced meat (pork and beef mix)**
- **generous amount of salt and pepper**
- **2 eggs**
- **3 slices of bread**
- **300 ml / 1 cup milk**
- **1 large onion**
- **oil**
- **flour**
- **butter (optional)**
- **dill, tomato and mayonez for garnish**

also needed:

- **big bowl**
- **pan**
- **cutting board & knife**

MAKE HANDS WET WHEN FORMING KOTLET TO PREVENT MEAT MASS FROM STICKING TO HANDS

watch the video

instructions:

1. soak bread slices in milk.

2. add minced meat to big bowl. add eggs.

3. cut onions in small pieces. heat up a pan. add some oil. add some butter (optional). fry onions until brown. add onions into meat and mix. by hand! add the soaked bread into the meat and mix again until combined.

4. form meat mass into balls and toss them in some flour. flatten them a little unless making giant meatballs.

5. heat up pan. add oil and butter. fry kotlet until brown on both sides and edges. remove heat and cover the pan with a lid for a few minutes.

6. serve with tomato on the side and of course mayonez for the full Boris experience.

7. let the dill rain from heavens and grant your wish of perfect taste.

Potato salad

pushing the limits

difficulty: Anatoli

prep: 1 h
cook: 30 min
chill: 1 h

ingredients:

- doctor's sausage
- potatoes
- carrots
- eggs
- canned peas
- pickles
- mayonez
- sour cream
- salt and pepper
- dill and green onion for garnish

since there is no legal limit to how much potato salad you can make I will not add amounts to this recipe. find the biggest container you have and start chopping!

also needed:

- pot for potatoes and carrots
- pot for eggs
- cutting board & knife
- bathtub for salad
- more people to help you chop

don't throw out potato peels !!! is good end of month snack

watch the video

instructions:

1. boil potatoes and carrots in big pot until soft inside. peel boiled potatoes. let cool down first or potato peel you.

2. boil eggs for 10 minutes until hard-boiled. when done pour out hot water and pour in cold water. this will make it easier to peel eggs.

3. get the biggest container you can find. cut everything into small cubes: doctor's sausage, potatoes, carrots, pickles, eggs (or just crush with hand).

4. finally add canned peas and preposterous amount of mayonez. also sour cream. don't forget salt and pepper! mix. mix. and mix some more. might need the strength of several Slavs to stir. depends how much salad you made.

5. time to dive in!

SLAVONIC GAMES

Black bread

with meat embedded

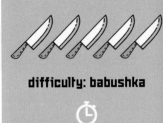

difficulty: babushka

prep: 3 days
cook: 40 min

ingredients:

- some kefir for starter
- 1 L / 4.2 cups water (40°C/100°F)
- up to 1.5 kg / 11.5 cups rye flour
- 4 tbsp sugar
- 1 tbsp salt
- 100 g / 0.3 cup bread syrup
- 4 tbsp malt flour
- 1 tbsp ground coriander
- some cumin seeds
- smoked ham (generous amount)
- cooking oil to lubricate the pan
- seeds (pumpkin, sunflower etc)

watch the video

also needed:

- jar
- big pot
- baking forms

instructions:

1. make the leaven by mixing some flour, water (40°C/100°F) and kefir together. leave in a warm place to come alive. this can take 1-5 days. the leaven is ready when small bubbles are rising from it.

2. add 1 L / 4.2 cups of warm (40°C/100°F) water to a big pot. pour in the leaven and dissolve. add some rye flour until you get consistency of thick kefir or light sour cream. leave in a warm place under a clean kitchen towel for 10 hours.

3. add sugar, salt, bread syrup, cumin, coriander and malt flour into the liquid dough. also add some seeds if you like. mix. add the rest of the rye flour in batches and mix well.

4. cut smoked ham in small cubes. mix into the dough.

5. oil two bread pans. do not fill more than half way with dough, bread will rise. cover with kitchen towel and leave in a warm place for 2 hours.

6. heat oven to 200°C / 400°F. bake the bread in the middle of the oven for 40 minutes until crust forms on top.

7. leave the bread to rest under a kitchen towel for 5 minutes before removing it from the form.

8. cut a celebratory slice of warm bread. eat with a thick layer of butter. congratulations! you have just made your own black bread!

Buterbrod

the Slavburger

difficulty: Vadim

🕒

prep: 3 min
cook: 0 min

ingredients:

- **bread**
- **butter**
- **doctor's sausage**
- **smoked sausage**
- **cheese**
- **tomato**
- **salt and pepper**
- **mayonez**
- **spring onion**
- **caviar (only on payday)**
- **cucumber**

also needed:

- **cutting board & knife**

IS BORIS'

instructions:

watch the video

1. take slice of bread.
2. put butter on top.
3. put everything else on top.
4. done! eat!

Classic

bread
butter
cheese
doctor's sausage

Classic+

bread
butter
cheese
smoked sausage
doctor's sausage

The End of the Month Special

bread
butter
cucumber
salt

The Boris Special

bread
butter
cheese
doctor's sausage
tomato
mayonez
green onion

The Slav Elite

bread
butter
caviar

Okroshka

with kuass

ingredients:

- **3 potatoes**
- **3 eggs**
- **1 long cucumber**
- **spring onion**
- **dill**
- **parsley**
- **6 small raddishes**
- **200 g / 7 oz doctor's sausage**
- **100 g / 0.5 cup sour cream**
- **1 tsp strong mustard**
- **1 tbsp mayonez**
- **1 tsp salt**
- **500 ml / 2 cups cold kvass**

also needed:

- **big bowl**
- **cutting board & knife**

watch the video

instructions:

1. boil potatoes until soft.
    cut into small pieces.

2. boil eggs until hard-boiled. slice.

3. peel and cut cucumber into small pieces. chop up green
    onions and dill. slice radishes. cut doctor's sausage into
    small pieces. add everything into a big bowl.

4. add generous amount of sour cream and mayonez, also
    some strong mustard and salt to taste.

5. finally add kvass. mix well. enjoy cold soup on hot day!

Pelmeni

tasty bags of meat

difficulty: Boris

prep: 1 h
cook: 7 min

ingredients:

dough:

- 250 ml / 1 cup water
- 1 egg
- about 300 g / 2.5 cups flour
- 2 tsp salt

filling:

- 250 g / 9 oz minced meat
- 1 small onion
- 1 clove garlic
- 2 tsp salt
- some pepper

also needed:

- bowl for dough
- bowl for filling
- big pot for boiling
- cutting board & knife
- rolling pin
- pelmeninator

instructions:

watch the video

1. into big bowl add egg, water and salt.
   whisk it all together. add flour and mix.
   with hands! mix until dough comes together.

2. take dough out of bowl and give it a Slav massage on
   lightly floured surface. knead for a few minutes. cover
   the dough and let sit for about 20-30 minutes. in the mean
   time make the filling.

3. cut onion and garlic into as small pieces as possible or use
   food processor. add into bowl with minced meat. add salt
   and pepper. mix. with hands!

4. roll out dough as thin as possible. remember to add flour
   to work surface so dough doesn't stick. use a drinking
   glass to cut out circles from dough.

5. put a teaspoonful of filling on the dough circle. fold and
   pinch edges together tightly. repeat until all dough and
   filling is used up.

6. put big pot of water to boil. use pelmeninator to put
   pelmeni into boiling water. not too many at once so they
   don't stick together. move them around with pelmeninator
   so they don't stick to the bottom. boil for about 7 minutes.
   after 7 minutes when pelmeni floats on top, scoop them
   out with pelmeninator.

7. serve with sour cream or mayonez for Boris way and let
   the dill fall from the heavens. enjoy!

Solyanka

great cure for cold or hangover

difficulty: Boris

prep: 30 min

cook: 65 min

ingredients:

- 2 L / 9 cups water
- 150 g / 5 oz doctor's sausage
- 200 g / 7 oz raw beef
- 150 g / 5 oz ham
- 4x small sausages
- 1 glass of pickle juice
- 4 pickles
- 1-2 onions
- 20 black olives
- 2 tbsp capers
- 3x potato
- 2x carrot
- 2x tomato
- 2x bay leaf
- 2-3 tsp salt
- dill and parsley
- lemon for garnish
- black bread for serving
- sour cream on top

also needed:

- big pot
- 2 pans
- cutting board & knife
- cold or hangover (optional)

watch the video

instructions:

1. cut beef into big cubes. put water into a big pot and boil the beef for 30 minutes. using the pelmeninator collect scum that floats on top and send it to neighbour Vadim.

2. cut doctor's sausage, ham and small sausages into small pieces. cut pickles, tomatoes, onion and olives into small pieces. grate carrots. cut potatoes into small pieces.

3. when beef is ready, cut into small pieces. keep meat water, it is soup base. put all meat produce and some oil on pan and fry until caramelized on sides.

4. fry onions and carrots on another pan for a few minutes. add tomatoes and pickles. cook for another 5 minutes.

5. boil potatoes in beef water for 15 minutes. then add meat mix and vegetable mix from pans into soup. add 1 glass of pickle juice, olives, capers, parsley and dill. and of course the bay leaf ... or two. add salt. boil for 20 minutes.

6. serve with sour cream, a slice of lemon and some black bread on the side.

Plov

perfect budget meal for student

ingredients:

- **300 g / 11 oz meat (pork, beef, moose, whatever)**
- **oil (sunflower seed for authenticity)**
- **300 g / 1.5 cups uncooked rice**
- **1 large onion**
- **salt**
- **3 carrots**
- **water**
- **1 whole garlic**
- **parsley for serving**

also needed:

- **1 pot**
- **cutting board & knife**

watch the video

RICE EXPANDS WHILE COOKING. USE BIG ENOUGH POT!

instructions:

1. cut meat into pieces. big or small - doesn't matter. add enough oil into the pot to cover the bottom. fry meat pieces.

2. cut onion into rough pieces and add into pot to fry until onions are soft.

3. cut carrots in half and then into quarter logs. add to pot.

4. meanwhile wash rice. add rice into a bowl and pour in cold water. stir until water becomes white and drain. repeat one more time. this removes extra starch and gives rice much better texture. set aside.

5. now back to the stuff frying in the pot. add salt and enough water so things are just covered. add one whole garlic into the pot.

6. after 10 minutes take out garlic. set aside for now. distribute the washed and drained rice in an even layer over contents in pot. do not mix! set heat to low. pour in rest of the water slowly so you don't mix layers of meat and rice. cook on low heat until water level is below rice level and add back the whole garlic. cook on low heat for 25 minutes or until rice is soft.

7. now it is time to finally stir the plov. serve with parsley and maybe some mayonez.

8. Eat!

Triple French pork

a hearty winter meal

ingredients:

- 500 g / 18 oz pork
- salt, pepper
- mayonez
- 1 medium sized onion
- 100 g / 4 oz cheese or more

> in absence of meat mallet use month old bread

also needed:

- cutting board & knife
- meat mallet
- grater
- oven pan

TENDERIZE MEAT FOR SOFTER TEXTURE AND FASTER COOKING

watch the video

instructions:

1. cut pork into thick slices.
    flatten all pieces with a meat mallet.

2. spread oil on oven pan. put one layer of meat in the middle
    of oven pan. sprinkle with salt and pepper.

3. cut onion into small pieces. prinkle onion pieces on meat.

4. add a layer of grated cheese on top of meat and onions.

5. spread a layer of good mayonez on top of cheese.

6. you could now put the pan in the oven at 180°C / 350°F for
    40-50 minutes. but if you want to make French pork the
    Boris way you keep going!

7. add a new layer of meat on top. sprinkle with salt and
    pepper. add onions again, cheese and top it all off with a
    generous layer of Slavic gold - mayonez! repeat process
    until you run out of meat. top the whole thing with a layer
    of grated cheese.

8. heat the oven to 180°C / 350°F.
    cook the French pork pile
    for 1.5 hours. serve with
    mashed potatoes and your
    favourite drink.

Herring under fur coat

cooking in style

difficulty: Boris

🕐

prep:	30 min
cook:	1 h 30 min

ingredients:

- 3 potatoes
- 2-3 beets
- 2 eggs
- 2 onions
- mayonez
- 1 large carrot
- herring fillet (smoked or salted)
- dill and parsley for decoration

smaller pieces
=
bigger flavour

watch the video

also needed:

- cutting board & knife
- deep plate or shallow bowl
- 3 pots

SHOCK EGGS
FOR
EASIER
PEELING

instructions:

1. boil beets in one pot. boil potatoes and carrots in second pot. stick knife in produce to check if ready. if knife comes out smoothly then is ready. drain.

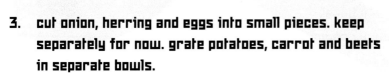

2. boil eggs in third pot until hard-boiled. shock boiled eggs by putting them in cold water. makes peeling easier.

3. cut onion, herring and eggs into small pieces. keep separately for now. grate potatoes, carrot and beets in separate bowls.

4. now start building shuba in layers: potato, herring, onion, mayonez, carrot, beet, mayonez again, egg.

5. finally sprinkle some dill and parsley on top and leave in the fridge overnight if have self control. enjoy pure Slavic goodness. dig in!

SHUBA SHOT
for a quick
pick-me-up

Christmas pork

super secret superslav recipe

ingredients:

- 250 ml / 1 cup pickle juice
- 50 ml / 0.2 cups sunflower seed oil
- 1 tbsp Estonian strong mustard
- 1 tbsp honey
- 1 tbsp mayonez
- salt and pepper
- 1 kg / 2.2 lb pork neck and belly
- bay leaf
- 2 small onions
- dill and green onion for top

also needed:

- cutting board & knife
- oven pot
- bowl for marinade

instructions:

watch the video

1. first make the marinade. in a bowl mix
    pickle juice, mustard, honey, oil and mayonez.

2. cut meat in big cubes and add salt and pepper. put meat in
    oven pot. pour marinade on meat. mix it around so all is
    covered. add the bay leaf ... or maybe two. cut onions in
    half and stick into the meat for best taste.

3. put the pot of meat in fridge to marinate overnight or less
    if already hungry.

4. take the pot out of the fridge an hour before cooking to
    let come to room temperature. if too hungry or in a hurry
    put the cold pot in the cold oven and heat oven up with
    pot inside. cold pot + hot oven = ruined holiday. who has
    money to buy new pot!? remember to cover the pot with a
    lid. cook in the oven at 200°C / 400°F for 2 hours.

5. enjoy with a side of boiled potato, fried fermented
    cabbage and pickle. some strong mustard on the side. let
    the dill and green onion fall from heaven like Christmas
    snow. cheers!

great leftover food. even better the next day

Holodets

Slavic meat jelly

difficulty: Boris

prep:	15 min
cook:	6-7 h
cool:	10 h

ingredients:

- **2-3 pork hocks**
- **1-2 pork feet**
- **enough water to cover the pork bits**
- **5 onions**
- **1 tbsp black peppercorns**
- **3 tbsp salt (or more if needed)**
- **2 tbsp sugar**
- **1 tsp grated nutmeg**
- **4 bay leaves**
- **6-7 cloves of garlic**

HOLIDAY SPECIAL

also needed:

- **huge pot**
- **pelmeninator**
- **bowls to put meat jelly in**

watch the video

instructions:

1. pay a visit to butcher Dima and get pork hock and feet.

2. add pork bits into a big pot and cover with water. bring to boil. skim off foam with pelmeninator for clean taste and clear jelly. add salt and sugar.

3. cut onions and garlic in half, peeling optional. add them to meat. simmer on low heat for 5h.

4. add peppercorns and grated nutmeg to meat. do not forget the bay leaf ... or 4! simmer for another 1-2h.

5. remove from heat and carefully take out the pork bits. pull the meat apart into small shreds. pour the broth through a sieve. set pulled pork back into the broth and heat it up again. add more salt if needed. remember, it will taste less salty when cooled down so make sure it is salty enough.

6. ladle the meat soup into separate bowls and leave to cool down in the fridge or cold pantry for 10 hours.

7. enjoy holodets with a side of strong mustard, vodka and black bread.

Piroshki

with salty or sweet filling

difficulty: babushka

🕐

prep: 1 h 20 min

cook: 30 min

ingredients:

dough:

- 50 g / 1.7 oz fresh yeast block
- 50 ml / 0.2 cups lukewarm water
- 100 g / 0.5 cups unsalted butter
- 85 g / 0.4 cups sugar
- 1/2 teaspoon salt
- 300 ml / 1.2 cups milk
- 600 g / 4.8 cups flour

salty filling:

- 400 g / 14 oz minced beef
- 1 tsp salt
- some pepper
- 1 boiled egg
- some boiled rice

sweet filling:

- 1/2 cup of jam
- 2-3 tsp potato starch

also needed:

- big bowl
- cutting board & knife
- 1 L / 4 cups sunflower seed oil for deep frying
- big pot
- pelmeninator

instructions:

1. set a pot of rice to boil.

2. now it is time to wake up the yeast.
   alarm clock not needed. add yeast into a
   big bowl. crumble it between your fingers for easier
   dissolving. add warm water - about body temperature.
   stir until yeast is completely dissolved.

3. melt butter in a cup and add milk. again make sure milk
   and butter mixture is not too hot or cold. too hot will kill
   the yeast and too cold will put it back to sleep. stick your
   finger in the milk and butter mix to test. if feels lukewarm
   is good. pour mixture into yeast bowl. add sugar and salt.

4. add flour little bit at a time. mix until dough comes
   together then continue kneading with your hands until
   dough is elastic and not so sticky anymore. form dough
   into a big ball and cover bowl with a
   clean kitchen towel. let rise for
   1 hour in a warm area.

watch the video

53

5.   in the mean time make the salty filling. cut onions into
     small pieces. fry on pan until light brown. add minced
     meat. add salt and pepper. fry until brown. put meat in
     blender and process until paste. put the paste into a bowl.

6.   in a small pot boil eggs until hard-boiled. peel eggs and cut
     into small pieces. add into the meat paste. also add cooked
     rice into the meat paste. why? because this is an excellent
     way to stretch your meat. *cough*. mix well.

7.   by now the dough should have doubled in size. take it out of
     the bowl and put on a lightly floured work surface. form
     dough into big sausage and cut into equal pieces. roll each
     dough piece out into a circle. put filling on top. fold dough
     over the filling and close ends in classic pelmeni style.

8.   if making sweet piroshki combine
     jam and potato starch in a small
     bowl. adjust starch quantity
     according to how runny
     your jam is.

for sweet
filling mix
jam with
potato starch

9. heat up oil in a big pot. there should be enough oil to submerge the piroshki. if making both salty and sweet piroshki, I suggest you make salty ones first in case the jam leaks. with pelmeninator carefully lower piroshki into oil - few at a time. do not crowd the pot. deep-fry until both sides are brown, 2-3 minutes. put on paper towel to cool down a bit. sweet piroshki jam will be hotter than chernoblin core.

10. serve salty piroshki with some mayonez and sweet ones with a glass of cold milk. feast!!

Crab salad

staple on holiday and birthday table

difficulty: gopnik

prep: 20 min
cook: 12 min

ingredients:

- **8 crab sticks**
- **quarter of a long cucumber**
- **50 g / 0.5 cup grated cheese**
- **4 boiled eggs, grated**
- **quarter of a small onion, diced or grated**
- **1 clove garlic, grated**
- **3 tbsp canned corn**
- **some salt**
- **4 tbsp of mayonez or more if needed**

HOLIDAY SPECIAL

watch the video

also needed:

- **big bowl**
- **cutting board & knife**

BREAKING NEWS

0% crab in crab sticks! suspect - white fish. crime wave exp...

instructions:

1. bring a pot of water to boil, add eggs and cook for about 12 minutes until hard-boiled.

2. cut crab sticks into small pieces. add into a big bowl.

3. add corn without water.

4. add cucumber cut into small pieces.

5. add grated onion and garlic.

6. add grated cheese.

7. add grated eggs.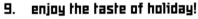

8. add an absurd amount of mayonez. then add some more. add salt aswell. mix.

9. enjoy the taste of holiday!

Kulebyaka

oooooooy it is good!

ingredients:

dough:

- 400 g / 3.2 cups flour
- 5 g / 0.2 oz dry yeast
- 1/2 tsp salt
- 2 tsp sugar
- 1 tbsp cooking oil
- 250 ml / 1 cup milk
- 1 egg

also needed:

- cutting board & knife
- bowl
- rolling pin
- pot
- pan

filling:

- 2 boiled eggs
- 100 g / 0.5 cup rice
- 500 g / 18 oz salmon
- green onion and dill
- 6-9 mushrooms
- 1 medium onion
- 50 g / 0.2 cup butter
- salt and pepper

Holiday Special

THE PERFECT LOAF

10/10

watch the video

instructions:

1. add flour and dry yeast into a big bowl. into a measuring cup add milk, salt, sugar, egg and oil. mix. add liquids into dry ingredients. mix until dough comes together. cover with kitchen towel and leave in warm place to rise for 1 hour.

2. sprinkle some salt and pepper on salmon and wrap it in alumininuminum. bake in the middle of the oven for 30 minutes at 180°C / 350°F.

3. make blins on the side. also cook rice and boil eggs.

4. cut up egg, green onion and dill in small pieces. set aside.

5. cut mushrooms and onions into not so small pieces. fry in butter until brown. add salt and pepper.

6. dough should now have doubled in size. put on lightly floured work surface and knead a bit. roll out into big rectangle shape.

7. layer fillings on the lower half of dough in following order: rice, mushrooms & onions, blin, salmon, greens, egg, blin. fold dough over the filling. cut off excess dough but leave a few cm of dough around filling to make the gopnik braid.

8. brush pastry with some raw egg and bake in the oven for 20 minutes at 200°C / 400°F.

9. serve with holiday spirit and mayonez for the Boris way.

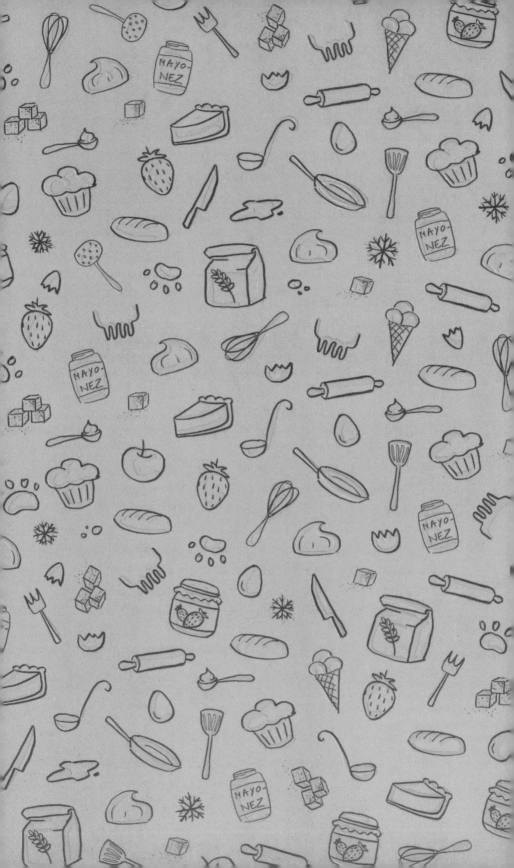

Mayonez ice cream

real winter treat

difficulty: gopnik

prep: 10 min
freeze: 3 h

ingredients:

- 200 ml / 1 cup heavy cream
- 100 ml / 0.5 cup cow juice
- 2 tbsp mayonez
- 70 g / 0.5 cup sugar
- 1 vanilla pod

also needed:

- bowl
- wooden spoon
- -20 cold outside
- or freezer

watch the video

instructions:

1. cut vanilla pod lengthwise in half and scrape out contents with a tool of your choosing — spoon, knife, axe...

2. mix all components in a big bowl. it is best if ingredients and bowl are already cold.

3. if you have ice cream machine, just throw the mixture in for 20 minutes. if you do not have ice cream machine then go outside and start mixing until done. if outside is not freezing temperature, put in freezer. take out every 15 minutes to mix.

4. if don't know what consistency to look for - ready ice cream feels like ... frozen heavy cream.

5. enjoy ice cold!

Babushka's jam

great on blins!

difficulty: gopnik

prep: 10 min
cook: 15-30 min

ingredients:

- 1 kg / 2.2 lb strawberries
- 1 kg / 5 cups sugar
- ...that's it

also needed:

- jars for preservation
- pot for boiling
- wooden spoon
- potato masher
- pelmeninator
- ladle

LASTS IN JAR FOR 2 years

* HAH! maybe at dentist's house

ONLY USE FRESH STRAWBERRIES!

watch the video

instructions:

1. start by cutting the stems off
    strawberries. slice each strawberry
    in half and throw into a big pot. attack the strawberries
    slightly with potato masher. do NOT use blender!

2. add in the sugar. put the pot on medium heat and boil for
    15-30 minutes. stir the jam often so as not to burn it. use
    a wooden spoon. when foam forms on top, remove it with
    pelmeninator. it is ready when less foam is forming. final
    colour should be dark red and not black.

3. jam is ideal when it drips slowly off the back of the
    wooden spoon. for long-term preservation sterilise your
    jars by boiling them.

4. ladle the jam into jars but leave some air room. preserve
    in a cool place or eat right away.

5. good luck!

cook longer
=
thicker jam

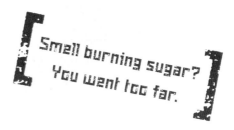

Smell burning sugar?
You went too far.

Boris' dream cake

the cake that never was

ingredients:

base:

- 50 g / 0.2 cup melted butter
- 100 g / 0.4 cup sour cream
- 100 g / 3.5 oz halva (sunflower seed best)
- 160 g / 6 oz soviet tea cookies (vanilla)

filling:

- 250 g / 9 oz quark
- 100 g / 0.4 cup sour cream
- 4 tbsp sweetened condensed milk
- some peel of lemon
- half a lemon's juice
- some milk chocolate

also needed:

- bowl
- spoon
- hammer to crush cookies with
- form to make cake into

refrigerate overnight if have self control

watch the video

instructions:

1. mix together halva and sour cream until blended. add crushed cookies and melted butter. mix until combined. put into a cake tin, spread evenly and refrigerate.

2. mix tvorog (aka quark, curd cheese, cottage cheese, farmer cheese), sour cream and condensed milk. add lemon zest and lemon juice. mix well. spread topping on the base evenly.

3. add chocolate shavings on top. let cool down in refrigerator.

4. follow your dreams. eat cake. stay cheeki breeki!

Blin

the mother of all desserts

ingredients:

- 100 ml / 1 cup milk
- 100 g / 1 cup flour
- 1 egg
- 1 tablespoon oil
- 2 tablespoons sugar
- 1 teaspoon salt
- oil for frying

eat blins with any filling you like - jam, mayonez, honey, garlic, ham, cheese, sourcream and caviar or all of them combined.

also needed:

- big bowl
- pan
- spatula

watch the video

instructions:

1. mix all ingredients together in big bowl.
    must be consistency of sour cream. if too
    thick add more milk. if too thin add more flour. easy.

2. heat up a pan. add oil. pour some of blin batter on hot pan
    so it creates a thin layer.

3. when one side is brown, turn blin over. cook until other
    side is also brown.

4. enjoy with a variety of fillings or as is.

Condensed milk blins

because blin is life

ingredients:

- **200 g / 1 cups sweetened condensed milk**
- **250 g / 2 cups all-purpose flour**
- **500 g / 2 cups kefir or regular milk**
- **1 egg**
- **1 tsp of salt**
- **1 tsp of baking powder**
- **oil for frying**

watch the video

also needed:

- **big bowl**
- **pan**
- **spatula**

instructions:

1. crack one egg into a bowl.

2. add sweetened condensed milk and flour. mix well.

3. add kefir (also known as buttermilk or sour milk).

4. add salt and baking powder. mix well.

5. heat up some oil on pan. ladle the batter onto the pan and fry on medium heat until both sides are golden brown.

6. enjoy with your favourite topping and a glass of kefir.

! never use water to put out oil fire! use metal lid, oven tray, salt, baking soda or fire extinguisher to smother the flames.

Frankenblin
a.k.a. Palacsinta

what the blin?!

difficulty: gopnik

prep: 5 min
cook: 15 min

ingredients:

watch the video

- 1 egg
- 180 ml / 0.75 cup milk
- 10 tbsp flour or more if needed
- 180 ml / 0.75 cup sparkling water
- 1/2 tsp salt
- 1 tsp sugar (optional)
- oil for frying

also needed:

- big bowl
- pan
- spatula

instructions:

1. in a suitable container mix together milk, egg, flour, salt, sugar and sparkling water. consistency should be runny.

2. heat up the pan and add some cooking oil. ladle enough batter to cover the bottom of pan in a thin layer.

3. fry on both sides until golden brown.

4. enjoy with sweet or salty fillings. stay cheeki breeki!

Slav spaghet

oodles of freaky noodles

difficulty: Boris

prep: 30 min

cook: 25 min

ingredients:

- **500 g / 4 cups flour**
- **2 eggs**
- **300 ml / 1.3 cup water**
- **50 g / 1.7 oz poppy seeds**
- **500 ml / 2 cups milk**
- **1 tbsp butter**
- **20 g / 0.7 oz raisins**
- **20 g / 0.7 oz almond flakes**
- **20 g / 0.7 oz chopped walnuts**
- **20 g / 0.7 oz sunflower seeds**
- **1 tsp vanilla sugar**
- **1 tbsp honey**
- **1 shot of rum or vodka**

also needed:

- **bowl**
- **rolling pin**
- **pot and pan**
- **spatula**
- **sieve**

instructions:

1. add flour, eggs and water into a big bowl. mix until it becomes dough. take it out of the bowl and knead on work surface until smooth and not sticky.

2. get your top of the range AK-Rolling Pinnovich ready. roll out dough into thin blin shape. cut into strips using knife. cut strips into bite-sized pieces.

3. rinse poppy seeds in a sieve. heat up milk in a pot. add poppy seeds. simmer for 20 minutes on low heat. strain poppy seeds. keep milk for drink later or use in blin.

4. melt butter on pan. add raisins, almond flakes, chopped walnuts and sunflower seeds. fry on medium heat until smells good. add poppy seeds, vanilla sugar, honey and a shot of rum or vodka. if mixture looks like gunpowder you're on the right path.

5. while the gunpowder simmers on the pan, boil noodles. bring a pot of water to boil and add some salt. put noodles into boiling water. stir so they don't form one big lump. boil 3-4 minutes. drain water and add noodles into gunpowder on pan. mix through.

6. eat!

watch the video

soak poppy seeds in milk overnight

Napoleon mini cake

smol kek

ingredients:

dough:

- 150 g / 1.2 cups flour
- 60 g / 0.3 cup cold butter
- 1/4 tsp salt
- 60 ml / 0.25 cups cold water
- 1/4 tsp 30% vinegar
- 1/4 egg

also needed:

- bowl for dough
- scale
- rolling pin
- pot for custard

custard:

- 375 ml / 1.53 cups milk
- 35 g / 0.17 cups sugar
- 2 eggs + 40 g / 0.2 cup sugar
- 50 ml /0.2 cup milk
- 20 g / 0.16 cup flour
- 1/2 tsp vanilla sugar

watch the video

instructions:

1. add 150 g / 1.2 cups of flour into a big bowl. add 60 g / 0.3 cups of cold butter and 1/4 tsp salt. squeeze mixture with your hands until it becomes small crumbs.

2. in a cup mix 60 ml / 0.25 cup of cold water and 1/4 tsp vinegar. pour into the dough and mix. add 1/4 of an egg into the dough. see video to learn how to extract 1/4 of an egg. mix well.

3. pour the dough out of the bowl and knead on a lightly floured surface for 3 minutes until it no longer sticks to your fingers. wrap the dough in cling film and put into the fridge to set for at least 2 hours.

4. after 2 hours it is time to start making the custard. add exactly 375 ml / 1.53 cups of milk and 35 g / 0.17 cups of sugar into a pot. heat up the mixture while stirring occasionally until steam starts to rise from the surface. do not boil! take the pot off the heat and set aside for now.

5. into a separate bowl crack two eggs and add 40 g / 0.2 cups of sugar. whisk by hand until mixture becomes pale and fluffy and your arm is numb. or use an electric mixer for about 5 minutes. add 50 ml / 0.2 cups of milk into the mix. also add 20 g / 0.16 cups of flour. mix gently until combined and no flour clumps are visible.

6. add the egg mixture into the pot with warm milk. add 1/2 tsp of vanilla sugar. set on low heat and keep mixing until custard is thick. this takes about 5-10 minutes, depending on the heat. custard should be smooth and not like scrambled eggs. if there are some lumps inside just push the custard through a sieve.

7. preheat the oven to 200°C / 400°F.

8. take dough out of the fridge and cut into 7 equal parts. roll out the pieces of dough. cut round shape out of each by using a cup. set leftover dough pieces on the baking tray too. you will use them for crumbs on top of cake. poke dough pieces with fork so they don't rise too much. bake for 5 minutes in the middle of the oven until golden brown.

9. cool down pastry layers and start building the cake tower, layering pastry and custard until you run out of both. top layer should be custard. break leftover dough pieces into crumbs and add on top and sides of cake.

10. refrigerate for a few hours or overnight to let layers soak in the custard.

11. congratulate yourself on succeeding to cook on max difficulty. new level of taste experience unlocked.

Zefir

best friends with tea

difficulty: babushka

🕑

prep:	30 min
cook:	15 min
dry:	48-72 h

ingredients:

- 1 egg
- 2 medium apples
- 300 g / 1.5 cups sugar
- 100 ml / 0.4 cups water
- pinch of salt
- 1 tbsp lemon juice
- powdered sugar
- 2 tsp thickening agent (gelatin, agar agar or pectin)

watch the video

also needed:

- pot
- sieve
- whisk
- big bowl for mixing
- measuring cup or scale

instructions:

1. peel and cut apples into small pieces. add them into a small pot. pour a little water in the bottom and cover with a lid. boil for 10 minutes on medium heat, stirring occasionally. cook until apple is soft and water has evaporated.

2. push cooked apples through a sieve with a spoon. add the apple sauce back into pot and add 100 g / 0.5 cups of sugar. heat until sugar has dissolved and sauce is thick. set aside to cool.

3. separate egg white and yolk (see video for tutorial). add egg white into a big bowl (save egg yolk for some gogol-mogol later). add a pinch of salt. add the cold apple sauce into the egg white. whisk until mixture is light and fluffy. add lemon juice if making it Boris style. mix. set aside.

4. add 100 ml / 0.4 cups of water and 200 g / 1 cup of sugar into a pot. add your choice of thickener (see video for more details). put pot on medium heat and keep stirring the syrup until it starts bubbling. boil for 5 minutes stirring constantly until mixture thickens. drizzle the hot syrup very slowly into the egg whites while constantly whisking. you do not want lumps of hard syrup in your zefir.

5. spoon the mixture into a piping bag. the piping hole of the bag should be quite big. push out favourable shapes of zefir on baking paper. not too small or too flat. leave to dry uncovered for 24-48h at room temperature.

6. once zefir has dried on the outside peel them off the baking paper. stick bottom sides of 2 zefirs together and roll in powdered sugar. leave to dry for an extra day. is ready when outside is crispy and inside is soft.

7. enjoy with tea!

Halva

sweet semichki brick

difficulty: Anatoli

prep: 20 min
cook: 10 min

ingredients:

- 200 g / 1.5 cups sunflower seeds
- 400 g / 2 cups sugar
- pinch of salt
- a little water to make sugar syrup

also needed:

- pan
- pot
- blender

instructions:

1. roast semichki on a pan on medium heat for about 5-10 minutes. keep tossing them around so they don't burn.

2. spread semichki on a big oven tray to cool down.

3. pour semichki into a food processor. process until it turns into paste. add a pinch of salt into semichki paste.

4. add sugar and a little water into pot. on medium heat cook until sugar has dissolved.

5. pour sugar syrup into semichki paste a little bit at a time. mix constantly until very thick.

6. put mixture in some kind of form - food container, baking tin etc. press down until compact. leave to set for 24 hours or eat immediately. enjoy!

watch the video

Chocolate sausage

not good on buterbrod

ingredients:

- 100 g / 0.5 cups melted butter
- 150 g / 5.5 oz vanilla cookies
- 1 tbsp sugar
- 2 tbsp cocoa
- marmalade candy
- 50 g / 0.2 cups sweetened condensed milk
- shot of vodka or rum (optional)

tastes much better than it looks

also needed:

- small pot for melting butter
- bowl for mixing

no access to marmalade candy? try raisins or dried sweetened cranberries instead. soak in rum beforehand for extra kick!

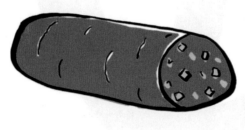

instructions:

1. melt butter.

2. pour the sweetened condensed milk into a big bowl.

3. crush cookies into crumbs. add into the condensed milk.

4. add sugar and cocoa powder.

5. cut up marmalade candy in small pieces and add to the mix.

6. add melted butter and an optional shot of vodka or rum. mix well until combined.

7. add the mix on baking paper and roll it up into a big sausage. put into the fridge to set for 1 hour or overnight.

8. cut chocolate sausage into slices and enjoy!

watch the video

Pavlova cake

no connection to Pavlov's dog
although some drooling may occur

difficulty: Boris

prep: 25 min
cook: 1 h (+1)

ingredients:

- 4 eggs
- 1 tbsp potato starch
- 200 g / 1 cup sugar
- 1 tsp apple vinegar or lemon juice (optional)
- pinch of salt
- 300 ml / 1.5 cups whipping cream
- 3 tbsp sugar
- strawberries
- kiwis

watch the video

also needed:

- big bowl
- mixer or whisk

instructions:

1. set oven to 200°C / 400°F.

2. separate 4 eggs. add egg whites into a bowl. keep yolks for gogol-mogol later. add 200 g / 1 cup of sugar and a pinch of salt. add 1 tbsp potato starch. using a mixer or hand whisk beat egg whites until stiff peaks form.

3. place baking paper on cooking tray. scoop whipped egg whites onto the paper in two mounds and with the back of a spoon shape into round cake bases. not too thin or they will crack. make a dip in the middle to hold more whipped cream later. turn oven to 150°C / 300°F and bake for 1h. then turn off heat, open the oven door a little to let moisture out. keep the door cracked open and let bases cool off in the oven for an extra 1 hour after turning off temperature. this makes pavlova crispy on the outside.

4. add whipping cream and 3 tbsp sugar into bowl and whip until fluffy. spread half of whipped cream on one base. make sure cake base is completely cooled down before.

5. add sliced kiwi and strawberries on top.

6. add second cake base on top. then add the rest of whipped cream and more strawberries and kiwis.

7. eat!

refrigerate for 1 hour for best result

Knedle

you can never have too many knedle

difficulty: Boris

prep: 30 min
cook: 10 min

ingredients:

- 10 small plums
- 5 small potatoes
- about 200 g / 1.5 cups flour
- 1 oval chicken produce
- 1 tsp salt
- a lot of sugar
- 100 g / 0.5 cups butter
- 50 g / 0.5 cups breadcrumbs
- some vanilla sauce on top

also needed:

- pot
- bowl
- rolling pin
- pelmeninator

watch the video

instructions:

1. boil some potatoes. peel after boiling
    to lose less material. put potatoes in a pot and mash.

2. add egg, salt and flour into potato mash and mix.

3. cut plums almost in half, leaving one side intact, and hide
    some sugar inside.

4. take dough out of the pot and put on floured work surface.
    knead. roll out the dough with rolling pin until thin.

5. cut dough into squares big enough to fit a plum inside. wrap
    each plum in dough and pinch edges together so it wouldn't
    unwrap while cooking. roll in your palm until smooth.

6. set water to boil in big pot. lower knedle in the boiling
    water using the pelmeninator. stir from bottom so knedle
    doesn't get stuck. cook for 10 minutes.

7. in the mean time fry butter, breadcrumbs and sugar on
    pan on low heat. set aside into a bowl.

8. fish out a knedle from pot and drop into the breadcrumbs
    mix. roll it around so crumbs stick to knedle.

9. serve with vanilla sauce or milk on the side. feast!

Gogol-mogol

the classic egg slurry

difficulty: Vadim

prep:	5 min
cook:	0 min

ingredients:

- **2 eggs**
- **2 tbsp sugar**
- **1 small tsp vanilla sugar**

also needed:

- **bowl**
- **whisk**
- **cup**

cheap & easy dessert

BEAT EGGS UNTIL LIGHT AND FLUFFY

instructions:

1. separate egg yolks from whites. save egg whites to make zefir later.

2. add sugar and vanilla sugar.

3. beat eggs until light in colour and foamy in texture.

4. pour into a cup of your liking.

5. enjoy simple and smooth dessert.

watch the video

Honey cake

more layers, more flavour

prep: 45 min
cook: 40 min

ingredients:

dough:

- 3 eggs
- 150 g / 0.75 cups sugar
- 1 tsp baking soda
- 400 g / 3.2 cups flour
- 4 tbsp honey
- 100 g / 0.5 cups butter

also needed:

- pot
- bowl
- rolling pin
- baking form

filling:

- 500 g / 2.2 cups sour cream
- 150 g / 0.5 cups condensed milk

watch the video

instructions:

1. in a medium-sized pot mix together eggs, honey, butter and sugar and heat up on low temperature. mix constantly, you don't want omelette. add baking soda and keep stirring. when mixture starts changing colour to brown take it off the heat and mix in flour in small portions. mix until all flour is incorporated.

2. in a separate bowl mix sour cream and condensed milk.

3. take out dough from pot and lightly massage. form into sausage shape and cut into 10 equal pieces. roll out dough pieces into thin round sheets. use your cake form to cut out the right size of cake layer. keep scraps for later, they will make crumbs for top and sides of cake.

4. heat up oven to 180°C / 350°F. line oven tray with baking paper and place dough circles on it. in the spare space add dough scraps. you won't fit all so bake in batches. bake each batch for about 6-8 minutes until golden brown but not burnt. keep an eye on it.

5. cool down layers completely before building cake tower. find a suitable plate and start constructing. cover layer of cake with a generous amount of cream. repeat until you run out of dough layers. cover top and sides with cream.

6. crush up baked dough scraps into crumbs and cover cake with it. for best taste leave in fridge overnight.

7. eat on birthday, holiday or just because you can.

Kissel

almost kompot

ingredients:

- 1 L / 4 cups fresh, frozen or dried fruits and berries
- 200 g / 1 cup sugar or more if needed
- 2 L / 8.5 cups water
- 6 tbsp potato starch

for topping:

- milk
- or ice cream
- or whipped cream
- or mayonez if Boris

also needed:

- pot
- pelmeninator
- ladle

add vodka
for extra
kick!

watch the video

instructions:

1. add fruit and water into a big pot. bring to boil.
   collect foam floating on top with pelmeninator.

2. add sugar and a pinch of salt.

3. put starch into a cup and add a little cold water. stir until
   dissolved. add starch into the kissel pot. mix until kissel
   becomes thick. take pot off heat.

4. ladle the kissel into containers of your preference. fancy
   glassware, bowls, cups etc. eat hot or cold.

5. serve with some whipped cream on top.

Thicclava

Boris' Balcan blin cake

difficulty: babushka

prep: 40 min
cook: 30-40 min

ingredients:

dough:

- 200 g / 1.3 cups pistachios
- 1/2 glass of warm water
- 220 g / 1.8 cups flour
- 1/2 tsp of salt
- 2 tbsp vegetable oil
- 100 g / 0.5 cup melted butter

syrup:

- 1/2 glass of water
- 1/2 glass of sugar
- 2 tbsp lemon juice

also needed:

- pot
- bowl
- rolling pin
- cake form
- brush for butter

instructions:

1. mix flour and salt in big bowl. add oil and half a glass of warm water. mix until dough comes together. knead on floured work surface until smooth. wrap dough in kling film and set aside.

2. make syrup. mix water and sugar in pot and bring to boil. add lemon juice. crush pistachios or process in blender until fine. melt butter in small pot.

3. cut dough into smaller pieces. roll it out as thin as possible. use your cake form to cut out circles of dough.

4. brush butter on bottom of cake form. add first layer of dough. brush butter on top of that. add another layer of dough. brush butter on top. repeat until have used up most dough layers. save 2 dough layers for top.

5. add crushed pistachios on the cake. spread out evenly. add remaining two dough layers. remember to put butter between them. using sharp knife cut through dough in X-formation so pieces have rhombus shape.

6. bake in oven at 180°C / 350°F for 30 minutes. take cake out of oven and pour syrup over the hot cake.

7. enjoy your thicclava!

watch the video

Syrniki

cottage cheese blins

difficulty: gopnik

prep: 5 min
cook: 15 min

ingredients:

- 400 g / 1.5 cups ricotta cheese
- 100 g / 0.8 cups flour
- 2 eggs
- 5 tbsp sugar
- 1 tsp vanilla sugar
- 1 tbsp vegetable oil
- 50 g / 0.2 cups soft butter
- 1 tsp salt

on top:

- sour cream
- condensed milk
- doctor's sausage
- cheese
- mayonez of course

also needed:

- bowl
- pan
- spatula

watch the video

instructions:

1. add all ingredients into a big bowl. mix.

2. heat up pan with oil. put big spoonfuls on syrnik dough on pan so that they are not touching.

3. fry on low heat for a few minutes on each side until golden brown.

4. serve with sour cream or any topping of preference.

NO WRONG WAY TO EAT SYRNIKI

Waffles

edible plates

ingredients:

- 200 g / 1 cup melted butter
- 200 ml / 0.8 cup milk
- 2 eggs
- 250 g / 2 cups flour
- 100 g / 0.5 cup sugar
- 1/2 tsp salt
- 1 tsp of vanilla sugar

for topping:

- 200 ml / 1 cup heavy cream
- 1/2 tsp vanilla sugar
- 2 tbsp sugar
- jam

due to high butter prices you may have to row beneath the black flag

also needed:

- bowl
- big spoon or small ladle
- old school waffle iron
- wooden spatula

instructions:

1. add dry ingredients into a big bowl.

2. melt butter and add it into the dry ingredients.

3. add milk and eggs. mix well until combined.

4. heat up the waffle iron. old school ones are best but newer ones will probably work too. spread some butter on the hot waffle iron. makes it easier to unstick the waffle later.

5. spoon some batter onto the iron. don't overfill. close the iron and cook for a few minutes. every iron is different so cooking times vary. peek at the waffle. if golden – is ready. unstick the waffle with a wooden spatula. if want to make cones roll up while it's hot and set aside to cool.

6. while waffles are cooking make whipped cream. add cold heavy cream (35%), sugar and vanilla sugar into a bowl and whisk until fluffy.

7. serve with whipped cream and jam or why not with mayonez ice cream!

watch the video

Chocolate cake

a'la Boris

difficulty: Anatoli

prep: 15 min
cook: 40 min

ingredients:

- 200 g / 1.6 cups flour
- 200 g / 1 cup sugar
- 150 g / 0.7 cup butter
- 150 ml / 0.6 cup milk
- 2 eggs
- 200 g / 7 oz dark chocolate
- 1.5 tsp baking powder
- 1 tsp vanilla sugar
- some almonds
- 1 tsp lemon juice
- 1/2 tsp grated lemon peel
- 2 tbsp cocoa powder (optional)
- 2 tbsp of espresso (optional)

CHEEKI-BREEKI CERTIFIED. BORIS APPROVES!

for topping:

- whipped cream
- berries of your choice

also needed:

- big bowl
- small bowl for chocolate
- spoon
- baking form

instructions:

1. break chocolate into pieces and put in a bowl. set bowl over a pot of hot water and stir until melted. in another pot warm up milk and butter together. set aside to cool.

2. whisk eggs and sugar until light and fluffy. mix together flour, baking powder and vanilla sugar. mix them into the whisked eggs. add milk and butter mixture into the batter. mix in chopped almonds, lemon juice and grated peel. you can also add cocoa powder and a shot of strong coffee for extra flavour.

3. grease the baking form with some butter and pour cake batter into the form.

4. bake at 175°C / 350°F for 35-40 minutes. check if ready by sticking a wooden toothpick into the center of cake. if toothpick comes out clean then is ready.

5. let the cake cool down. decorate with a lot of whipped cream and top with berries.

watch the video

American apple pie

western spy tart

difficulty: Boris

⏱

| prep: | 2 h |
| cook: | 1 h |

pie crust:

- 300 g / 2.5 cups flour
- 1 tbsp sugar
- 1 tsp salt
- 230 g / 1 cup cold butter
- 7 tbsp very cold water

> as seen from video,
> the American recipe was
> a bit...um...extravagant
> for my taste. here is a
> modified version.

filling:

- 6-7 apples (sour kind are best)
- 80 g / 0.4 cup brown sugar
- 80 g / 0.4 cup white sugar
- 1 tbsp lemon juice
- 1/4 tsp fine salt
- 1 tsp ground cinnamon
- 1/4 tsp grated nutmeg
- 3 tbsp butter
- 2 tbsp cornstarch
- a bit of milk to brush pastry

also needed:

- bowl
- cutting board & knife
- rolling pin
- baking form

instructions:

1. mix flour, sugar and salt in a big bowl. cut cold butter into cubes and add to the dry ingredients. using your fingers pinch the cubes of butter until everything is combined into a crumbly dough. add ice water one tablespoon at a time and mix gently with fingers or fork. don't knead.

2. form dough into balls and then flatten into disks. wrap each in plastic wrap and place in fridge for at least 1 hr.

3. let cold dough rest at room temperature for 20 minutes. on floured surface roll both dough disks thin. flip the dough during rolling so it doesn't stick.

4. use rolling pin to transfer one dough sheet to pie dish and other one on baking paper or floured tray. put both in the fridge to cool down while you prepare the filling.

watch the video

PERFECT PRESENT
FOR NEIGHBOUR VADIM

5. preheat oven to 200°C / 400°F.

6. mix together dry ingredients and spices in a small
    bowl. set aside.

7. slice apples (peeling optional) into a big bowl. add lemon
    juice, soft butter and dry ingredients and spices.

8. pour apple filling into the pie dish. gently press down
    the apples to make sure filling is tightly packed.

9. cover the pie with the second layer of dough. cut off
    overhanging pie crust around the dish. flute the edges,
    which is just fancy speak for "make wavy edges".

10. cut some holes into the top crust to let steam escape during baking. brush the pie with some milk and place in the oven.

11. bake for 1 hour. if pie seems to brown faster on one side you can turn it around during baking.

12. let pie cool down so it is not boiling.

13. enjoy with vanilla sauce or ice cream and a cold glass of premium cow juice.

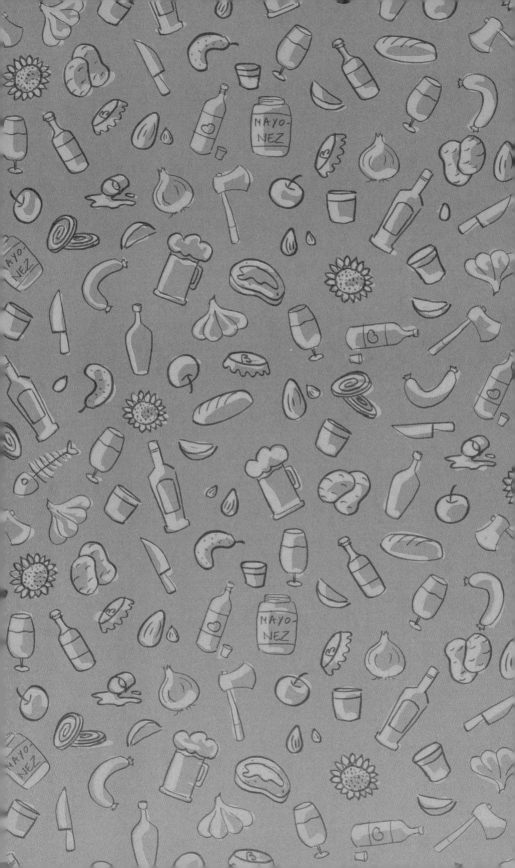

Garlic blackbread

the Slav popcorn

difficulty: Vadim

prep: 10 min
cook: 10 min

ingredients:

- **rye bread**
- **garlic**
- **salt**
- **cooking oil**

also needed:

- **pan**
- **cutting board and knife**

instructions:

1. cut bread into bite-sized pieces.

2. heat up a pan, use plenty of oil. add bread on hot pan and fry until crispy. put fried bread into a pot or bowl.

3. crush garlic or cut into small pieces and add into the fried bread. add plenty of salt. place a lid on top and shake well.

4. enjoy with mayonez dip or as is.

watch the video

Doctor's sausage

dr. Boris approves

difficulty: Boris

prep: 30 min
cook: 45 min

ingredients:

- 110 g / 4 oz pork (cold)
- 20 g / 0.7 oz beef (cold)
- 20 g / 0.7 oz pork fat (cold)
- 40 ml / 0.16 cup milk (cold)
- some ice (for extra cold)
- 1/4 tsp ground black pepper
- 1/4 tsp ground nutmeg
- 1/2 tbsp salt
- 1 tsp sugar
- 1/2 egg
- beet juice or red food dye

also needed:

- sausage skin
  or plastic wrap
- some string
- kitchen thermometer
- piping bag
  or sausage machine
- a blender
- pot

instructions:

1. cut up cold pork, beef and pork fat into pieces. add into the blender. throw in some ice cubes to keep mixture cold. process until minced.

2. pour milk into a jug. add salt, pepper, sugar and half an egg. grate some nutmeg. mix until sugar is dissolved.

3. use thermometer to measure temperature of the meat mix. it should be below 15°C / 59°F. pour some of the milk mix into the meat mix. process until combined. add the rest of milk mix and process again until smooth.

4. put meat paste into a piping bag. tie up one end of the empty sausage skin and roll up the other end. start piping meat paste into the sausage skin gradually to avoid air bubbles. when sausage is filled tie up the other end.

5. heat a pot of water to 80-85°C / ~ 180°F. cook the sausage for about 45 minutes. take sausage out of water and let cool.

6. enjoy on buterbrod or just as snack!

watch the video

Bublik

the Slavic bagel

ingredients:

- 25 g / 1 oz fresh yeast
- 2 eggs
- 150 ml / 0.6 cup of water
- 250 g / 2 cups of flour
- 1 tbsp sugar
- 1 tbsp salt
- poppy seeds for topping

also needed:

- bowl
- ladle
- big pot

116

instructions:

1. dissolve yeast in a little bit of warm water. crack two eggs into a bowl, add salt and sugar. mix. add dissolved yeast, 150 ml / 0.6 cups of water and 250 g / 2 cups of flour. mix until dough comes together.

2. pour the dough onto a well floured surface. knead until dough is elastic and no longer sticky. divide the dough into 4 balls. if you want to add any flavourings inside, do it now. flatten the dough ball, add flavourings and knead back into a ball. leave dough balls to rise under a clean kitchen towel for about 30 min.

3. bring a big pot of water to boil. poke a hole in the middle of the dough ball with your finger. expand the hole *ahem!*. throw dough hoop into the boiling water or lower it using a spatula if not wearing a welding mask. boil for 30 seconds on each side.

4. cover oven pan with baking paper. place boiled bubliki on it. if using, add toppings, for example poppy seeds, coarse salt or semichki. bake at 180°C / 350°F for 12 minutes.

5. enjoy with cream cheese or any topping of choice.

watch the video

Salt-brined pickles

when life gives you cucumbers, make pickles!

difficulty: Vadim

prep: 15 min
marinate: 24 h

ingredients:

- 1 L / 4 cups water
- 2 tbsp salt
- 10 small cucumbers
- 4 blackcurrant leaves
- 2 grape leaves
- 1 horseradish leaf
- 1 dill umbel
- 3 garlic cloves

also needed:

- pot
- big jar

watch the video

instructions:

1. cut ends off small cucumbers.

2. set a pot of water to boil and add salt. for every liter of water use 2 tbsp of salt. you can add more salt if you like. taste for measure.

3. put cucumbers into jar with the fresh blackcurrant, grape and horseradish leaves. also add dill umbel. it is the flowering part of dill plant. cut garlic cloves in half and add into the jar.

! you can also add hot peppers or spices to your liking

4. once water comes to a boil, take it off the heat. pour hot water on top of the pickles in the jar. water should cover everything. seal jar tightly with lid.

5. wait at least 24h.

6. enjoy.

use fresh produce. Limp cucumber won't make crispy pickle

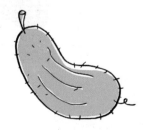

Russian cheese

processed cow juice

difficulty: babushka

prep: 3 h
mature: 4 weeks

ingredients:

- 3 L / 13 cups milk
- 1/4 tsp cheese starter culture
- 1/4 tsp calcium chloride
- 15 drops of rennet
- salt
- 1 uncracked egg for salt test

1 L milk
=
100g cheese

also needed:

- big pot
- kitchen thermometer
- pelmeninator
- colander
- cheese cloth
- cheese form
- cheese wax

watch the video

instructions:

1. pour milk into a big pot and heat it up to 33°C / 91°F. use a cooking thermometer to get temperature right.

2. sprinkle the cheese starter culture into the milk and stir gently with pelmeninator. cover with a lid and set aside for 30 minutes.

3. dissolve calcium chloride in just a little bit of water. pour it into the milk pot and stir.

4. dissolve 15 drops of rennet in 100 ml / 0.4 cup of water and pour into the milk. mix well. cover with a lid and set aside for 45 minutes.

5. milk should have solidified by now. run a long knife through the curds to cut it into small pieces. stir gently with pelmeninator. leave to rest for 5 minutes. the curds will sink to the bottom.

6. remove 1/3 of the whey (leftover cheese water). in another pot heat up some water to 55°C / 131°F (about the same amount as the whey you removed). add warm water to the curds. mixture should be about 38°C / 100°F now. mix. repeat this step one more time.

7. place a cheese cloth on top of colander and strain the curds. wrap cheese cloth over curds and shove it into a cheese form. the form should have holes so water can drain. add 5 kg / 11 lb of weight on top to squeeze out excess water. after 20 minutes take out the cheese, flip it over and put it back into the form. leave it under 10 kg / 22 lb of weight for 6 hours.

8. time to salt the cheese. add a lot of salt into a bowl of water. put an egg into the water. if it sinks, add more salt. if egg floats, is salty enough (make sure your egg is fresh. rotten eggs also float). add a little calcium chloride in the water, it will make cheese more hard on the outside.

9. add the cheese block into the salt water. add some weight on top to keep it submerged. leave cheese to salt for 6 hours on one side then flip it around and salt for 6 hours on the other side.

10. take the cheese out of the water and leave to air-dry for 3 days at 15-20°C / 60-68°F temperature. flip the cheese once every day for better drying.

11. melt cheese wax in a pot. dip the cheese in hot wax until all sides are covered. leave to mature for 28 days.

12. enjoy 28 days later.

watch the video

Pashtet

make you strong!

difficulty: Boris

prep: 30 min
cook: 40 min

ingredients:

- **500 g / 18 oz pork liver**
- **1 L / 4 cups milk (optional)**
- **1 tbsp salt**
- **1/2 tsp pepper**
- **bay leaf**
- **1/4 tsp nutmeg**
- **100 g / 3.5 oz pork fat**
- **1 large carrot**
- **1 large onion**
- **150 g / 0.7 cups butter**
- **parsley for decoration**
- **1 tbsp diluted vinegar**

also needed:

- **cutting board and knife**
- **pot**
- **pelmeninator**
- **meat grinder**
- **container for pashtet**

KEY TO SMOOTH PASHTET
IS PLENTY OF BUTTER

instructions:

1. place liver in milk for 2 hours (optional).

2. cut liver into smaller pieces, about 5-10 cm / 2-4 inches and add into a pot with water. set to boil for 20-30 minutes removing foam as it appears. at the same time cut pig fat, carrots and onions into small pieces and fry them together on a pan. after about 20 minutes of boiling the liver, cut up one piece and see if ready. if it is still pink in the middle boil for another few minutes.

3. slice up cooked liver into smaller pieces and add to the pan with other components. add grated nutmeg and of course the bay leaf ... or maybe two. fry for 2-3 minutes until mixed well.

4. pick out the bay leaves and grind mixture in meat grinder or food processor. add butter for smoothness and vinegar for flavour. add salt and pepper to taste. mix well and grind again.

5. package into favourite container. decorate with parsley.

6. enjoy!

watch the video

Mayonez muffins

... a'la Anatoli

difficulty: Anatoli

prep: 20 min
cook: 10-15 min

ingredients:

- 240 ml / 1 cup cow milk
- 2 big tbsp of good quality mayonez
- 125 g / 1 cup flour
- 2 tsp baking powder
- 1/2 tsp salt
- 400 g / 14 oz minced meat
- 1-2 medium onions
- 1-2 cloves garlic
- some salt and pepper to taste
- cheese (as much as you like)

try also:
bacon
smoked chicken
salmon
...

also needed:

- cutting board and knife
- bowl
- pan
- grater
- muffin pan

watch the video

instructions:

1. put flour into a big bowl. add mayonez. pour in milk. add baking powder and salt. mix well.

2. make filling. cut onion and garlic into very small pieces.

3. heat up pan with oil. fry minced meat, onion and garlic until brown. don't forget salt and pepper and ... the bay leaf.

4. grate the cheese.

5. let minced meat cool down a little and add it into the dough. also add grated cheese. mix.

6. grease the muffin pan. spoon dough into the muffin holes. sprinkle more cheese on top. bake in the oven at 180°C / 350°F for 10-15 minutes.

7. done!

Potato peels

end of month fine dining

difficulty: gopnik

prep:	15 min
cook:	10 min

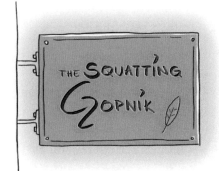

watch the video

MENU

THE CLASSIC

oil coated potato peels with salt and pepper
baked in oven at 200°C for 20 minutes

THE PUB WAY

deep fried potato peels with salt and pepper
served with garlic mayonez and pickle on the side

THE FULL MEAL

pan fried potato peels
with butter sautéed onion and garlic
spiced with rosemary, salt and pepper

THE CLASSIC +

oiled potato peels with chives, salt and pepper
baked in the oven at 200°C for 20 minutes
served with sour cream and green onion

THE SIBERIAN BEAR

potato peels pan fried in pig fat
spiced with bay leaf and salt

THE PROFESSIONAL

potato peels presoaked in vinegar and water solution
dusted in flour and deep fried until golden
coated in secret herb mix

THE SURPRISE

deep fried potato peels
with sugar and honey

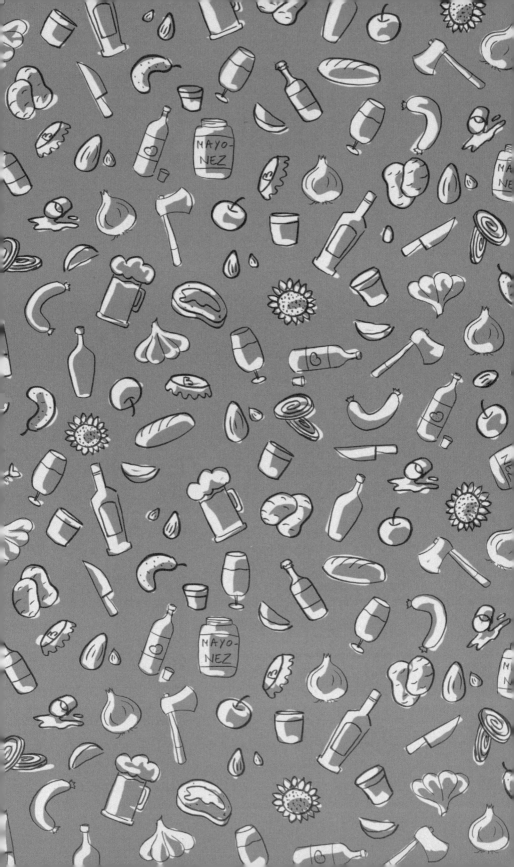

Gopnik beer

for every Slav occasion

difficulty: Boris

🕐

prep: 30 min
brew: 7-14 days

ingredients
for whole container:

- 5 kg / 25 cups sugar
- 20 L / 5.2 gallons water
- 5 kg / 1 gallon malt extract
- 50 g / 2 oz yeast

ingredients
for much smaller container:

- 500 g / 2.5 cups sugar
- 2 L / 8.5 cups water
- 500 g / 1.5 cups malt extract
- 20 g / 1 oz yeast

watch the video

also needed:

- container to make beer
- long spoon for stirring
- cup

the longer you brew the stronger the beer

close valve tight unless want to join gopnik space program

instructions:

1. thoroughly clean your container.
   you will need one that withstands pressure.

2. mix water, sugar and malt extract. stir until dissolved.

3. in a cup mix yeast with some sugar until it turns liquid.
   add yeast mix into the rest of components.

4. close the container loosely to let air escape. let mix sit at
   room temperature but not in direct sunlight for 24h.

5. after that, close container tight
   and let sit for 7-14 days.

6. drink.

if contents look like sewage water you're on the right path !

[Don't drink and drive
then all is fine!]

Apple juice

liquid vitamin for long winter

difficulty: gopnik

prep: half a day
cook: 15 min

ingredients:

- **apples**

also needed:

- **bucket to wash apples in**
- **shredder**
- **wooden stick for poking**
- **juice press**
- **pot**
- **jars for storing juice**

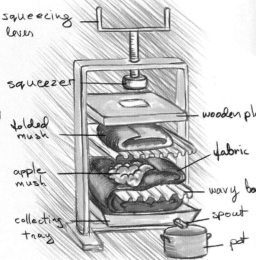

squeecing lever

squeezer

folded mush

apple mush

collecting tray

wooden pl

fabric

wavy bo

spout

pot

instructions:

1. collect apples from garden. wash off dirt.
   throw apples into grinder. poke with stick if needed.

2. spread shredded apple mush on fabric sheets in juice
   press. fold sheet over the mush like an envelope. place
   wavy board on top. add another layer. on very top add
   wooden plate.

3. spin the squeezing lever until juice starts running. have
   pot ready to collect it! the squeezed out apple mush looks
   like big blin ... but is not. throw it out.

4. heat up apple juice on the stove. with pelmeninator collect
   scum that floats on top. bring to boil and take off heat.
   pour juice in sterilized jars.

watch the video

5. enjoy all year round!

Top secret Boris invention

patented household multitool autumn special

Kompot

more than fruit floating in water

difficulty: Vadim

prep: 2 min
cook: 30 min

ingredients:

- **blueberries**
- **strawberries**
- **cherries**
- **3 L / 13 cups water**
- **2 tbsp honey**
- **1 large cup sugar**
- **1 lemon**

kompot is foundation of true Slav childhood. didn't have it growing up? make extra kompot as therapy.

also needed:

- **big pot**
- **ladle**

hot kompot
for winter

cold kompot
for summer

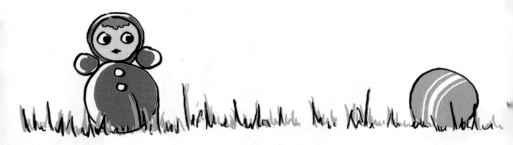

watch the video

instructions:

1. collect fruit from garden or supermarket.

2. heat a big pot of water until boiling.

3. add fruit into the boiling water. bring to boil again and then lower heat to not boil over.

4. add honey and sugar. stir.

5. after 30 minutes take pot off heat. add juice of 1 lemon.

6. add kompot to jug for immediate consumption of Slav essence or store in jars for winter.

Kvass

not just a drink - is lifestyle

difficulty: Anatoli

🕐

prep:	30 min
ferment:	2 days

ingredients:

- 1.5 L / 6 cups water
- 1/3 cup of raisins
- 1 tsp dry yeast
- 100 g / 0.5 cups sugar
- 2 slices of black rye or pumpernickel bread
- 1 lemon

also needed:

- pot
- sieve
- pelmeninator
- cotton cloth
- hermetic jars

watch the video

instructions:

1. add water to big pot and bring to boil.

2. toast black bread in toaster.

3. when water is boiling turn off the heat and add bread slices into pot. wash raisins and add those into pot aswell. if you like lemon, add some lemon slices too. cover with lid and let sit for 3 hours.

4. scoop out solid matter from pot using pelmeninator. pour liquid through sieve into another pot.

5. add some new raisins, sugar and yeast. stir. pour mixture into clean hermetically sealable glass jar. leave in a warm place for 2 days.

6. kvass should be bubbling nicely now. pour through a cotton cloth (cheese cloth or clean kitchen towel. NOT an old t-shirt) into a clean glass jar. add some lemon juice. seal the jar and place in fridge to cool down.

7. enjoy cold!

Don't drink and drive then all is fine!

Gopnik wine

for sophisticated gopniks

difficulty: gopnik

prep: 5 min
ferment: 1-2 weeks

ingredients:

- 1.5 L / 0.5 gallons jar of home made apple juice
- 200 g / 1 cup sugar
- 25 g / 1 oz fresh yeast (or 6 g / 0.2 oz dry)

instructions:

1. pour 400 ml / 1.7 cups of apple juice out of the jar into another container. pour sugar into the jar with apple juice. add in yeast. close lid.

2. shake! shake until sugar and yeast are dissolved.

3. yeast starts producing CO2 so open the lid a little to let out growing pressure or use an airlock. check video for more info on airlocks.

4. leave in warm place (~ 25°C / 77°F) for 1 week or longer to ferment. the longer you wait the stronger the wine.

5. cheers!

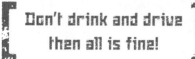
Don't drink and drive then all is fine!

watch the video

Mead

make with friend, drink with friend

ingredients:

- **3 kg / 9 cups honey**
- **20 L / 5.3 gallons water**
- **1 packet of mead yeast (or wine yeast)**

also needed:

- **big container with lid**
- **long spoon**
- **airlock**

watch the video

VOL 1

instructions:

PHASE 1

1. make sure all your tools and containers are clean.
    add water and honey into a big container with lid.

2. dissolve yeast in some warm water. add to container.

3. close lid and make sure to use airlock. you do not want
    explosion. leave in warm place for 2 weeks.

PHASE 2

4. after 2 weeks it is time for racking. it means siphoning
    off the clear mead away from the crap in the bottom.
    using a sterilized tube or a hose, siphon clear liquid into
    new container. do not let hose go too low and pick up
    sediment. once clear liquid is transferred, close the new
    container with lid. do not forget the airlock.

PHASE 3

5. wait for about 1 week until airlock stops bubbling. use
    a clean tube or hose to transfer mead into bottles. wait
    another few months if have self control.

6. drink with friends or give away as present - finest quality
    superslav artisanal mead.

watch the video

VOL 2

Boris' kitchen dictionary

pelmeninator - skimmer

chicken produce - egg

health stick - cucumber

eggbird - chicken

cow juice - milk

alcohol free vodka - water

potato juice - vodka

raw vodka - potato

alumininuminum - tin foil

pig bits on stick - shashlik

compressed cow juice - butter

processed cow juice - cheese

liquid bread - beer

AK-Rolling Pinnovich - rolling pin

Made in the USA
Columbia, SC
02 September 2024

e2b1dfef-23da-4573-bb8f-90f8857689b5R01